Blog Wonderful:
A Blogger's Guide To Success

Dana Fox

Introduction

During my first year of blogging, I put my heart and soul into creating and documenting what worked, and what didn't in terms of growing. The Wonder Forest blog is my baby, my pride and joy. It is the place where I can let it all out. Where I can be creative, and where I can share my thoughts and discoveries with the world. My blog grew pretty quickly during only the first six months, but it was not without hard work.

Blog Wonderful is a book designed for both the beginner and novice blogger that shares my own tips, tricks, and knowledge that was gained as a "new girl on the scene" during that first year. What you will find in this book is a collection personal thoughts about becoming better at blogging, taking your blog to the next level, as well as some helpful hints from my past profession as a web designer and internet fanatic. Whether you are looking to start a blog, or just want some help for your current one, I have you covered! I only know what has worked for me, and I hope that what I share will work for you too.

I thank you for joining me on this blogging journey, your support is so appreciated, you have no idea.

Dana Fox
thewonderforest.com.

What Others Are Saying...

"As a brand new blogger, I found Blog Wonderful to be a lifesaver! I learned SO much from design to commenting to advertising to things I never would have thought about or known before! This book is VERY well organized, so it's easy to navigate and also very easy to read. It has so many little details that only an experienced blogger could know and is willing to share. I felt like Dana was talking to me as a friend and helping my blog become more successful like hers. You can really tell that Dana put a lot of time and thought into this book. I really can't say enough good things about Blog Wonderful! I just finished the book today and I already feel like a more knowledgeable and confident blogger. Blog Wonderful is a great resource and I plan on revisiting it regularly!"

Michelle - sewingrocks.blogspot.com

"I absolutely love Dana's book, Blog Wonderful! Even though I've been blogging for awhile now, there were still so many great tips that I found extremely helpful. Everything from little design tips to how important it is to connect with your readers. The last chapter about making money with your blog has been a huge help! The tips I've found in Blog Wonderful have really helped to make sure I'm moving in the right direction. I'd definitely recommend this e-book to any new blogger!"

Sarah - www.simplydove.com

"I wasn't sure if I wanted to buy this book or not when I first came across it... But I am SO glad that I did! Not only has it given me a lot of awesome tips but it has really inspired me to be a better blogger and best of all.. to be MYSELF. I think that Dana is such a real person, I love her blog, her style and her shop so I knew that she would have intriguing and useful info to share, and she definitely did! What I have enjoyed most about Blog Wonderful so far is Dana's urge to not just follow the crowd of bloggers but to do what feels right to you. Since I started reading this, I've been more inspired to write which has led to more views and followers. I love the blog format and I find myself reading through Blog Wonderful daily. Thank you Dana!"

Tia - sewcalmama.blogspot.com

"Blog Wonderful has been an excellent resource for me and my fledgling little blog. From post layout tips to how to utilize social networking to planning your posts properly. She holds your hand through every step, and makes it easy to understand. I think the best part for me was the gentle reminder to just be yourself and share your life (or your business or whatever you're blogging about). Good things will come when you're genuine. And Dana, the Wonder Forest, and Blog Wonderful are truly genuine. A killer investment that you won't regret."

Jackie - perchedup.blogspot.com

CONTENTS

Chapter One
Getting started with your blog: Define yourself

I started blogging in the summer of 2011. One of the initial struggles I had was figuring out how I wanted my blog to **sound**. Did I want it to be business-oriented, did I want to share my personal life? How did I want my readers to view me? This is something that will probably take the most thought, because it is important to establish your voice and motives in order to succeed in the blogging world.

What you will first need to figure out is how you will be read. Do you want to write to your readers in the same way that you would talk to your friends? Or are you trying to stay professional if you own a business blog? Your writing style is important because it helps define your blog and future content. If a reader feels comfortable with your writing, they will come back. Some of my favourite blogs have a great writing style which is easy to read and makes me feel as though they're right there, in my own head, telling me their stories.

If you have never tried your hand at writing before, you might want to take some time to develop your own style before you jump into blogging. This is totally optional, but if you have no idea where to start, the best thing to do is practice. Get yourself a private journal and start writing about your day. As you start documenting things in your journal, your own writing style will start to take shape. I also find that reading books has helped me develop that "little voice in my head", which is the same voice I use when writing my blog, and much the same way this book is written.

Deciding on the type of blog you want to create is also an extremely important task. A niche blog will allow you to choose a specific topic and stick with it, whereas a personal blog will be a place of many subjects. Think about what you enjoy in life and go from there. Concentrating on topics that appeal to you or allow you to share your own expertise in certain areas can attract like-minded visitors.

Write down a main category that your blog would fit into and what you are trying to achieve.

A word of caution before you begin: If you decide to share your personal life with your readers, you need to be aware of the fact that **this is the internet**. Once you put something on the internet, it's there for good. It is not just a small group of people who will be browsing your blog; it's strangers, search engines, archive database websites, sharing sites like Pinterest, and even maybe your next door neighbour. Be certain that you're comfortable with what you share, and realize that just because your blog may be a "lifestyle" blog, that doesn't mean you have to share every private detail of your life.

Set limits for yourself right from the very beginning and decide what you will and will not talk about. There are a couple of things that I have personally put into my "off limits" vault that I just do not need the whole world knowing. Be sure to set these limits for yourself from the very start, and stick to them.

Now, let's get to the fun stuff!

Content

After you've taken the time to define your blog, you'll need to consider the type of content will you share. Make a list of everything you want to include and everything that interests you, and try to focus on the top three topics if possible. This will help to further categorize your blog and give you a little direction. For example, although I consider my blog a "Lifestyle" blog, that category in itself is SO broad. Your lifestyle might be totally different from somebody else's lifestyle. I could instead define my main blog topics as: Blogging, Inspiration, and Creativity. These three things help describe my blog quickly, and give readers an idea of the main things I post about.

What would you tell a stranger if they asked you what your blog was about? I don't cover celebrity gossip, because I'm not an entertainment blog. I don't write about babies, because I am not a mom and don't have a family blog. If you have too many things going on, your blog will not fit into a certain category and your readers might feel a little lost. *"Hey, I visited this blog to check out the latest DIY project and now all I see are posts about Ryan Gosling...?"*

Figure out what type of blog you want to be and the content will start moving! One of the hardest tasks I faced was defining my blog categories, but when I settled on them, I just knew they were perfect.

Always be yourself. I cannot tell you how your blog should sound or what kind of content you should have on it. These things will be entirely based on who you are as a person. Remember, your blog is always a reflection of who you are in some way. Don't choose topics to write about just because other bloggers are writing about them. Finding your voice and showcasing your skills is all about showing the blogging community who YOU are. There are no rules for this, as we are all different and none of us live the same life. I think that however you define yourself, as long as it is genuine, will contribute to your blog's success. You just have to actually believe in what you are writing about and make sure your writing style portrays who you are as a person or a business.

Getting Started With Your Blog: Where To Go?

With the internet being as vast as it is, there are many different blogging platforms to choose from. Blogger, WordPress, Typepad, and Tumblr to name a few. The majority of this book focuses on Blogger and Wordpress, but the tips still hold true for other platforms.

Blogger

Blogger is the most commonly used free blog platform and probably the easiest to handle straight out of the gate. It has everything you need to start your blog, and you can also set it up with your own custom domain name by following the tutorial on my blog located at www.thewonderforest.com/blogger-domain.

Blogger is not a self-hosted blog, which means that everything you create on it is stored on Google's servers. You never have to worry about website hosting fees, maxing out personal bandwidth, or hosting files (although, you cannot create your own custom email address through Blogger). They even make it easy to integrate Google Adsense with your blog and offer some pretty handy customizing tools.

Since Blogger is a part of Google's own products, they have SEO (search engine optimization) covered! You don't have to worry too much about fiddling with keywords because it is already set up for you.

Blogger has a handful of useful widgets that you can integrate with the click of a button, although you cannot add third party plugins as you can with some other blogging platforms, like WordPress.

You can also easily back up your blog though using these simple steps I wrote about on the Wonder Forest blog: www.thewonderforest.com/blog-backup. Backing up your blog should be a regular routine that you get yourself into, especially if you post often!

WordPress

WordPress offers a free online hosted version at www.wordpress.com and a self-hosted version for custom installs located at www.wordpress.org.

The self-hosted version is the one that I always recommend, but it means that you need to purchase your **own domain and hosting plan** from a hosting provider. For a complete guide to setting up your own Wordpress site in 5 minutes at a super affordable rate, visit www.thewonderforest.com/5-minute-blog.

Self-hosting your Wordpress blog means that you have more control over the features and design than if you were to use their free online hosted version which does not allow custom themes, edits, or the use of advertisements. You can also set up a custom email address through your hosting control panel to match your domain name.

WordPress, though it offers a lot of extra add-ons and features, can be a little tricky for newbies to customize, so look into downloading a theme that you like if you're not skilled with template editing.

There are definitely some advantages to owning a self-hosted WordPress blog. If you do know what you're doing, or you take the time to learn the system, the customization capabilities are endless. There is a mountain of WordPress plugins that can be installed onto your site such as galleries, SEO tools, social networking tools, and so much more.

To get your own Wordpress blog started for just $3.49/month, including a free domain name visit www.thewonderforest.com/5-minute-blog.

Getting Started With Your Blog: Making Time.

This is probably one of the most important aspects to blogging if your goal is to take your blog to higher levels or eventually create some sort of income from it. Blogging is a great hobby, but what if you want to make it more than a hobby? If you don't have the time to dedicate to it, stop right here, go back to the beginning, and re-evaluate why you want to blog in the first place.

If you have a bustling family and no time to even get dinner together, how will you be able to manage a blog? I am generally on my blog for about 1-3 hours every single day. That sounds crazy, right!? I agree it does, but I'm all about staying on top of things! Tweaking, editing, posting, networking, making my blog the best it can be. It essentially is a part-time job.

Blogging takes time. Not just the time it takes to write the blog post, but to also consider the following:

- Blog post topics
- Taking photos
- Uploading photos
- Editing photos
- Writing the post
- Proofreading the post
- Tweaking the post
- Publishing or scheduling the post
- Social sharing and promotion

As a blogger, these things will all become important to you, so make sure you have the time set aside. Decide how often you will post on your blog. Will it be every day? Every second day? Twice a week? Make sure whatever you decide can be **easily manageable for your lifestyle**. Personally, I try to leave my weekends post-free because it just doesn't fit with my schedule to post then.

Scheduling Posts

Blogger and WordPress both offer you the option to schedule your posts to be published on a certain date, at a certain time. Become familiar with this option because indeed it is a handy one!

If you have a free moment to knock off a couple of blog posts in a row, the scheduling features are priceless. In Blogger, you can access the scheduling options by clicking that little "Post Options" link beside the text editor. Set your Post date and time to "Scheduled at" then choose your date and time! Clicking Publish will save your post for that scheduled time and it will automatically post to your blog then.

Finding time to fit in a blog post or two in a day isn't always an easy task, but with the right discipline you can do it!

Timing of Posts

I always like to post around the same time each day. This isn't necessary, but I find it helps me stay on top of my blog. I like to post in the morning so that my blog post is visible all day long for anybody who wishes to come for a visit. I find that posting at night time and then again in the morning only lessens the time the visitor has to view that first post. This is totally a personal preference so whatever works for you may be different.

Once you figure out a blogging schedule that does work for you, it will just come naturally. Whether that means using any free time you have during a day to write up a new post, or planning in advance. Just remember that if you want to be successful, you need to put in the time!

Getting Started With Your Blog: Expectations.

What are your expectations for your blog? Do you just want to be able to share your thoughts with the world? Or are you hoping to offer a helping voice to a community of blog readers? Are you simply blogging just to make money?

This short chapter is all about your expectations for your blog. It's good to have goals for any project you take on, and blogging is no different. How realistic are your expectations though?

"I expect my blog to draw in a community of like-minded people."

That is a great **goal**, but do not **expect** it to just happen.

Like anything, building a following takes a lot of work, and people will not just find you and automatically become regular readers of your blog. You need to work for it, sister! Blogging and growing a following takes a lot of work. Do you think that some of the "bigger" bloggers just sit around all day watching the traffic pour in? Of course not, silly! If you want to attract a community of like-minded people, you'll need to get out there and put the work in!

"I want to have paid advertisers or use Google Adsense."

Great! However if you are just starting out, I am sorry to say, there is nothing for you to offer your advertisers. If you don't have a following built up and good traffic to back you up, you can't expect anyone to dish out money on your blog for sponsorship spots or advertising. What would be the point? How would that benefit them in **any** way? Expecting to make money right off the bat is completely unrealistic and *simply won't happen*. If you choose to utilize Google Adsense, don't expect to be making "free money" just by simply pasting their advertiser codes on your blog. I will share more about how Google Adsense works in the Adsense chapter!

Do not confuse expectations with goals. Goals are things you strive towards and realize that they don't come easily. Expectations can be unrealistic things that you think are just going to automatically happen without putting

11

forth any effort. So start making some real goals for yourself, and work towards them!

Getting Started With Your Blog: Branding.

Branding yourself is a must. First and foremost, choose a unique name for your blog. Your name should be easy to remember and easy to spell. This will be one of the most important decisions of your blogging career, because normally when you pick a name, you're stuck with it.

This name will be visible in your blog URL, your blog header, your social networking profiles, and all other marketing material, so make sure you choose one that you can live with!

If you have a blog and a shop, think about how you can combine the two should you need to. They could complement each other, have the same general theme, or perhaps a shared word.

If you need help with coming up with the perfect blog name, check out the video I created at www.thewonderforest.com/blog-name which shares my very own process for regularly coming up with project and business names.

Once you've come up with the perfect name, think to yourself: *Can I see this name in a heading/ on business cards/ in a URL? Is it catchy and memorable and easy to pronounce?* Once you have your name set, you're on your way!

What not to do: Don't choose a blog URL that doesn't contain your actual blog name. A reader has to be able to remember your URL just as well as your name. It is easier to remember a blog name such as "Danielle's Diary" with a matching URL such as **daniellesdiary.blogspot.com**, or **daniellesdiary.com**, than it is to remember that the blog "Danielles' Diary" is located at a different URL like **daniellelikesoranges.blogspot.com**. Simple enough, right?

Getting Started With Your Blog: Design.

In case you didn't know this, design plays a huge role in attracting visitors. As a professional web and graphic designer for over 10 years, I can absolutely vouch for this and have seen stats rise for my clients after a simple site re-design.

Blogger offers a "Template Designer" which is an easy way to customize your blog. If you want to learn the basics of Blogger and the Template editor, check out this video at www.thewonderforest.com/blogger-walkthrough.

This is all fine and dandy, but what if you want to be a little more original? You want stand out! You want people to take notice and think "Hey, this blog is really nice!"... don't you?

Firstly, if you have no design experience, do not fret. There are people who can help you out. If you're really truly considering making a great blog, the decision to hire someone or at least purchase a professionally created template should come easily. If you want to tackle this yourself and have some Photoshop or editing and coding experience, by all means go for it!

Your design can honestly make or break you. I can't count the times that I've visited a poorly designed blog and simply clicked "close" without even reading the content. If I'm doing it, you know others are doing the same thing.

So what constitutes a "good" design? You don't have to have all the bells and whistles, just some simple structuring of content and a nice clean feel will do the trick. Let's talk about what makes a good design...

Colours

Choose colours that are visually pleasing. This means no *lime green* backgrounds, red text, or crazy colour combinations. An easy way to think about colour is to picture paint swatch cards in your mind. Or heck, go and grab some paint swatches if you're in the mood! Paint swatches can usually easily be paired up with coordinating shades, and guess what? You can then use those matches as inspiration for your blog design!

When I'm designing someone's blog for them, I always ask them if they had any specific colours in mind, or what their favourite colours are. This answer usually comes easily for most people... because really, who doesn't have a favourite colour?! A colour palette is all you need to start customizing your blog.

Now, think about the overall *feel* of your blog. Think about what your blog is trying to convey. Does it have a certain theme? (Sewing, family, animals?) What do you want it to *feel* like? (Light and airy, bold and modern, shabby chic?). Choose a style that matches the topics you write about! This should give you a great jumping off point when combined with your chosen colours.

Feelings, nothing more than feelings...

Think about the feel of your blog. By this, I mean think about what your blog is trying to convey. Is it a certain theme? (Sewing, family, animals...). What do you want it to *feel* like? (Light and airy, bold and modern, shabby chic...). This should give you a great jumping off point when combined with your chosen colours.

Header Design

Headers for a blog are important because they are the first thing people see when landing on your page. They should set the tone for your entire blog, yet not overpower the whole site.

You'll want to make sure that your header includes your blog name as well as a tag line if you have one. A tag line just kind of summarizes what your blog is about, so the visitor knows what they're getting into.

If you don't have Photoshop, there are some online editing tools you can use to piece together a nice header. Photobucket has some new photo editing features that could do the trick, and Pixlr.com is a Photoshop-like online editor that I always recommend to others!

It really does pay off to invest in Photoshop, the world's most popular image editor. They have a Creative Cloud subscription service now that allows you to download both Photoshop and Lightroom for just $9.99 per month. Visit www.thewonderforest.com/adobe to download a free 30 day trial!

Tip: Your header shouldn't take up extreme amounts of space. It should be as wide as the entirety of your blog's content area (shown in image below). No larger, no smaller. I find that blogs with headers that are too small width-wise can really throw off the whole look of a blog. Headers that are too "tall" can also discourage readers. It's no fun to have to scroll down half a page to get to your content. Your content should be visible as soon as someone lands on your blog.

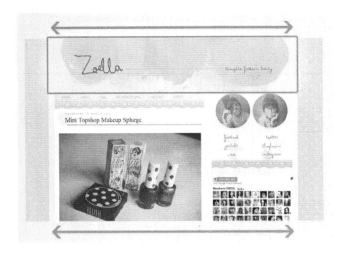

Content Area

The **content area** is everything below your header, where your content all resides (shown in below image). Content areas usually consist of a main post area and a sidebar. It is completely up to you how you want to arrange this section. Some people have one sidebar, some people have two, some have none. You can easily position them in Blogger's Template Designer, or choose a WordPress theme that appeals to you.

Your main post area should be wide enough to hold nice, large photos. Large, crisp photos are the key to making your blog feel pulled-together and professional. Your photos in your post area should always be the same width, stretching from one side of the post area to the other. This keeps things visually intact and is much more pleasing on the eye than if you were to have tiny photos centered in the middle of your post.

Your blog content area (outlined in below photo) should be the same width as your top header. Content areas that are too wide and stretch the entire width of the screen are bad for two of reasons:

1. They looks messy.

2. People with smaller screen sizes will actually have to scroll over to view all of your content.

Keep screen sizes in mind when organizing your blog. Normally I only make pages from 960px wide to a maximum of 1200px wide. Many computers have different *screen resolutions*, which means that what you see on your monitor might not be what someone else sees on theirs. If their screen resolution is smaller than yours, and your blog is a whopping 1600px wide, you're unknowingly causing them to have to scroll over horizontally to view your entire blog's contents. Keeping these within standard screen resolution sizes will benefit everyone.

Sidebar Content

So often I see sidebars with so much unnecessary clutter. Do you really need to put a button in there that says that you were featured on someone's link party? Use a separate page for that. Putting the most important content near the top of your sidebar is always key. What do you want people to see as soon as they land on your blog? Maybe this includes links to other social networking sites, or a link to your shop? People shouldn't have to scroll down your page to find the most important information from you, instead, it should catch their eye right away.

Don't fill it up just to fill it up. I have a hard time with my sidebar because even though it includes only necessary things, that I need to have visible, I sometimes still think it's too cluttered. I reorganize and remove things every so often to keep it fresh and clean it up. Cleaning up your sidebar should be done often and kept updated to avoid clutter and outdated content.

Music

Music or playlists on your blog should never be set to auto-play. This is pretty much a #1 rule in the web design field, and it is also important to remember when creating a blog. It is a huge disadvantage for blog owners who automatically have music playing when you visit their sites. Firstly, a reader might be at work when they check out your blog, and the last thing they need is for their speakers to start pumping out beats, immediately causing them to click the "close" button on their browser hoping that nobody heard. Secondly, not everyone may enjoy your musical taste. It can be a distraction for many while reading, and trying to find your little music player on your blog to hit "stop" is just too much of a hassle.

Overall, your blog should portray who you are. If it doesn't, try again! When you find that perfect combination of colour and feeling, it will come easily.

Getting Started With Your Blog: Photos.

I wanted to dedicate an entire section to photos because I

think they are super important. We talked about extending your photos the width of your content area in the last section, so now we will talk about your actual photographs.

Taking Your Own Photos

First, you need a camera. You don't have to have a fancy-dancy top of the line DSLR or anything like that. A simple point and shoot will do, you just have to know how to use it. Study your camera, read the manual, look up helpful tips and tutorials online so that you have a good understanding of how it works. As you start taking more and more photos, you might consider upgrading later on. I use a Canon Rebel T3i with either a 50mm lens or a 28mm lens. The 50mm lens is the cheapest of its kind (only around $130) but is more or less a blogger staple! It has tons of awesome reviews online. It really helps obtain nice, crisp images and has a great depth of field, which is how you get the out of focus background stuff to look blurred!

When taking your photos, keep the overall style of your blog in mind. If you're showcasing a certain product or item, take close-up shots! Learning how to use the Macro feature on your camera is a great way to get comfortable with extreme close-ups.

Make sure that item is the main focal point in the frame. Background distractions or other items shown in the frame that are not related to your post just take away from the object being shot. If you can't quite get close enough or eliminate some of the background distractions, you can always crop a photo in an editing program.

UP CLOSE AND CROPPED

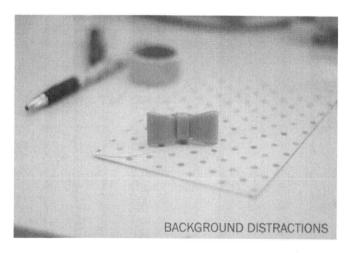

BACKGROUND DISTRACTIONS

Tip: Try to use natural light whenever it is possible. Natural light allows the object's natural colours to shine through. Using a flash on your photos is a classic mistake as it totally washes out the whole setup. Learn how to set your camera for different lighting situations. .

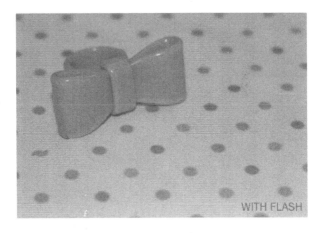

WITH FLASH

You should learn to take your own photos, especially if you are reviewing something or writing a how-to or a recipe post, for example. Using stock images or photos found on the brand's website is just not as genuine. You also have to worry about the photos not being the proper size for your content area as we discussed. Lastly, **don't use unnecessary photos**. Only use the ones that best represent what you're trying to convey. Your readers don't need to see five different shots of the same thing, at the same angle. It increases blog load times as well and takes away from the writing!

Using Found Photos

If you do choose to use photos taken by other people, always credit the original source. Crediting another blog that took the photo from somewhere else is not crediting the original source. Sometimes you have to click through a few different sites before you find the actual source, but you're doing everyone a favour and stopping the ongoing sourcing problem in its tracks.

In some of my posts I'll use inspirational photos, or photos of other lovely things found online to compliment the story. A lot of these images come from Pinterest, which is fine, but it's so important to give credit where it is due. You can include links to the photo sources in smaller lettering directly under the photo, or you can even put the credits at the bottom of your post... that is up to you. If you are unsure if you should use a photo, ask the photographer for permission.

Uploading Your Photos

In Blogger and Wordpress in particular you can upload your photos right in the editor. These images are hosted on your own blog once uploaded. All you need to do (in Compose mode) is click on the photo icon at the top of the editor, like so:

Clicking that pressed down button beside "link" will open up the Blogger uploader. There will be options along the left hand side that let you upload your own photo, add a photo from another URL, add one "From this blog" which is one you've previously uploaded before, as well as a couple other options. Choose to do a basic Upload and then choose your file. It will upload it and you can preview it in that window. Click on it and then choose Add Selected to add it to your post. Easy!

Sizing Your Photos

The best way to size your photos is to resize them in an editing program to match the width of your content area. If you cannot do that, you can use your blog editor's functions to scale them.

In Blogger, when you upload an image into your post, all you need to do is **click on it** in the editor to bring up a little text menu below it. You will see a couple of size options in there: Small, Medium, Large, Extra Large, and Original Size. Clicking on any of these will resize your photo. By default, Blogger creates different sizes of your image when it uploads. By clicking one of those links, you are swapping out one size for another. Extra Large usually works well on blogs. The width of the Extra Large option is 640px, so as long as your post area is 640px or a tiny bit bigger, your photo will look just fine. Otherwise, you can manually resize your photo in Photoshop or another editing program to your own custom size and click the "Original Size" link. A lot of bloggers are unaware of this setting, and it really does make all the difference in how your posts are displayed! WordPress also has its own settings for this.

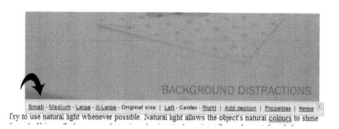

Small - Medium - Large - X-Large - Original size | Left - Center - Right | Add caption | Properties | Remove

Try to use natural light whenever possible. Natural light allows the object's natural colours to shine

Getting Started With Your Blog: Formatting Posts.

Formatting your posts is also something that should be done properly. Being in the design field, I am pretty OCD about having everything look consistent, so I thought in this chapter I could give some helpful tips about making your posts pretty!

We talked a little bit about having nice, large images in

your content area, but what about the rest? Text is just as important as images and shouldn't be overlooked.

Fonts

The fonts used in your posts should be the same throughout your entire blog. There is no need to use the post editor to change your font if you have already created your template design. Your template design uses a CSS file, which is basically a place where your entire blog's font characteristics, design styles, and much more are stored. When you set your post text in Blogger's Template Designer (for example, if you set the post font to Arial and a size of 12px), that information gets saved to your main CSS file, which means that ALL of your posts will use that same information. All of your posts will already have the font set to Arial, 12px.

I see a lot of blogs choose different fonts for their posts within the editor and it just tends to look messy and unorganized... Inconsistent, really. Try to keep these uniform throughout your whole site... It's much more visually pleasing for a reader.

Text Alignment

Next I want to talk about text alignment. Blogs that center all of their text drive me insane! Nobody reads a book, for example, that has centered text all the way through. It's harder to read, and our eyes don't naturally want to follow along. Left aligned or left justified text will help your blog read more like an article, or a book, than a mish-mash of words strangely aligned. I realize that this has sort of become a "trademark" way of blogging for many, so this is just my own opinion on the subject.

Paragraph Spacing

Lastly, let's jump into paragraph spacing. Sometimes when you're writing a blog, weird things can happen to paragraphs. Too many line breaks happen often. Even though it looks like you may have only pressed the "enter" key twice to form a nice new paragraph, for some reason there is double the amount of space. What gives?! That's just some good old wonky editor work at its best!

What I do before I preview my post, is view the HTML mode of the editor. This is where you will see if you have too many spaces in between paragraphs, and where you can fix them. If using Blogger, change the editor settings in the sidebar of your post to use the Enter key as a paragraph break, instead of the <br> option.

There should only be **one** blank space between your paragraphs, so in HTML mode, make sure that's the case before publishing.

Important note: Always, ALWAYS preview your posts
before you publish! You never know what your post looks
like until you do this, as you can't just rely on an editor to
figure it out for you.

Getting Started With Your Blog: Stats.

Some people say that numbers aren't important and that
they shouldn't define you. I agree that you shouldn't let
numbers define you, but I very much disagree that they
aren't important!

If you're taking this blogging thing seriously, you need to
stay on top of your stats. The same goes for any website
you're running. You can look at stats in two ways - you
can dwell on them and compare yourself to other blogs, or
you can see them as **goals**. I prefer the latter.

If you haven't set up a stat tracker, get on that! The most popular is Google Analytics, and it really does give you all of the stats you need. You can sign up quickly and easily over at the Analytics site (google.com/analytics).

Once you sign up, you will need to place a tracking code on your blog, which Google explains how to do. In Blogger, you either paste the code directly into the HTML of your template design, or you can take the easy way out and create a new HTML/JavaScript widget and paste it in there. When this is installed, Google will start collecting all of your data... usually it takes a day or so to start collecting.

Some things you'll want to look at are the following:

Users/Unique Visitors - This is the number of individual visitors who have visited your blog. It doesn't track every single click or refresh they make, which makes it a better tracking tool than Pageviews number.

Pageviews - Pageviews are the number of times your pages were loaded for a given time. Every time a unique visitor clicks a link and views a new page, that is a pageview. This number is usually much higher than your unique visitors count for this reason.

Both of these statistics will continue to let you know how much traffic your blog is receiving, which is very important if you ever consider offering any type of advertising on your site. In Analytics, you can view your stats per day, month, year, or even hourly.

Traffic Sources/Referrers - This is the place where you can check out where your visitors are coming from. It's very helpful to know this, especially if you are advertising your blog on other blogs. You can see how many unique visits you've received from certain websites, and even what people search for on Google when they stumble upon your site. You can also see how much "direct traffic" you received, which is when people enter your URL in their address bar instead of finding you someplace else.

Those are the very basics in the world of statistics, and the ones that I check the most often. If you're interested in growing as a blog, you need to stay on top of your stats and see how you can improve. It's fun watching your daily visits grow, and it also gives you a sense of accomplishment when you can actually see what you're doing paying off. Does that mean you should let your stats "define you"? Absolutely not! But I think it's important to see if what you're doing is contributing to making your goals a reality.

Chapter Two
All Set, Now What?
Social Networking

Welcome to Chapter 2! This chapter is all about what to do after you've launched your blog.

Now that you've got your blog started and it's designed nicely, it's time to start putting your hard work into action. Networking is the next step and one that should definitely not be overlooked.

Social media plays a key role in being found on the internet. There are millions of blogs online, and you've got to fight to make yours noticed. So get into the ring and let's get started with Facebook.

Facebook

Facebook is **essential** now-a-days, especially if you own a business or a blog. It's database where millions and millions of users can be tapped into and new fans can be found.

Start by signing up for a Facebook Page if you haven't yet. Facebook Pages are different from the standard personal profiles and are tailored just for people like you! There is no personal information shared with your fans and with the introduction of Timeline for Facebook Pages, you can design your Facebook page to match your blog!

One thing to remember when signing up for a Facebook page is that you'll want to get your own custom URL. For example, mine is www.facebook.com/wonderforest. By default, Facebook does not choose this URL for you. **You have to manually set it**.

If you weren't prompted when you signed up, to set your custom URL visit www.facebook.com/username. Here, there is an area where you can choose your own custom "Username" for your Page, if it's not already taken. Pick something that is in line with your blog name so it is easy to remember. Your URLS on all of your social media sites should be cohesive.

Playing around with Facebook will show you that the possibilities are enormous. It is such a great place to interact with your current and potential readers.

Facebook also offers some cool widgets you can add to your blog. If you visit their Social Plugins page, you can grab a cool "like" box and other goodies to add to your blog's sidebar.

Twitter

Twitter is another must-have for any blogger. Just like Facebook, there are millions of users on Twitter. You don't want to miss out on any opportunities to interact with anyone, so being on both networks is a good idea.

If you don't want to have to worry about constantly updating both sites, you can link up your Twitter profile to your Facebook page by visiting www.facebook.com/twitter, so that whatever you post on Facebook gets copied to Twitter. This is insanely helpful if you don't plan on being on Twitter all the time.

Bloglovin'

Bloglovin (www.bloglovin.com) is a feed reader for bloggers, with so much more. Their database of users consist of other bloggers from a variety of different categories like Lifestyle, Fashion, Crafts... the list goes on.

Many people use the site as their main source of finding all of the latest posts from their favourite blogs. You should sign up and create your profiles as soon as you're ready to network. Remember to choose the appropriate category for your blog when you do so!

What You Should Not Do

Social networking is not for spamming. In fact, you will **lose** followers for over-posting or posting useless nonsense. I try to limit the links I share so that people don't get annoyed with me. It's also important to not just use your accounts as a way to try to get people to your blog.

Take the time, interact with people, and be genuine about it. Others know when you're not being sincere or if you are just trying to get them to "follow you back" and it makes you look like that's all you care about.

All Set, Now What?
Comment Networking

What the heck is comment networking? It's a great way for other people to find your blog! The truth is, you will not be found in this gigantic world of bloggers if you do not get out there and visit other blogs. Become involved in the blogging community as a whole, but always, ALWAYS be genuine about it.

After you read someone else's blog post, leave a comment on it. Bloggers love comments, it's a fact. At the end of your comment, include a link back to your own blog, so that the blog owner, or even their readers who check out the comments can visit you. This absolutely **does** work and is a huge part of how I gained a lot of readers in the early stages of Wonder Forest.

The absolute worst thing you can do to another blogger is to leave a comment along the lines of *"Check out my blog"* or *"I followed you, follow me back!"*. I'm sorry, it doesn't work like that. First of all, it is so obvious when somebody leaves a comment and hasn't even bothered to read the blog post. Secondly, comments such as the examples above are spam. Yep, those are considered spam. Do you want to be known as a spammer blogger? I didn't think so. ;). When you leave a comment with your link in it, it's important to not be too "in your face" about it. My comments usually look something like this:

"Wow, I can't believe that you got that for only $10! I'm so jealous... the only place I've found a deal like that was at a garage sale, haha!"
xo Dana
thewonderforest.com

See the difference? My link is small, and it doesn't say things like "Enter my $300 giveaway now!" or "Follow me back!" A simple link is all you need as a sign off. For reference, the HTML code for a link like mine looks like this:

```
<a href="http://www.thewonderforest.com">thewonderforest.com</a>
```

While you're on that comment page, take a look at some of the other comments. Usually you can click on a name and be directed to their Blogger profile or website. From there, you can check out their own blogs too, and leave more comments! This is a great way to be introduced to new people and you may even find some new fav blogs!

Try to reply to people who comment on your posts. This shows that you've read their comment and appreciate them taking the time to share their thoughts.

Get out there and explore the blog world, there are a lot of great people to meet! Remember, it's not all about *you* and *your* blog, it's about **connecting** with this awesome network of blog buddies and supporting each other.

All Set, Now What?:
Quality Over Quantity

When thinking about your blog post topics, always remember one thing: quality over quantity. Don't post something just because you want to have a new post every day. If you can't come up with any decent ideas to write about one day, don't post at all. Filling your blog up with random articles that don't necessarily relate to your blog very well will confuse your visitors. Some people have an easier time with coming up with blog topic ideas, while others tend to hit road blocks often. That's ok! Don't force it. Your readers will be able to tell and your blog won't feel as genuine.

Tip: I find that the posts that get the most reactions are ones where I am being real, expressing my emotions or thoughts. People relate with emotions. It helps them to see that there's a real person behind that computer screen.

Posting something that is not in keeping with your overall blog can be a downfall in itself. Always make sure that your content comes first and remember why you want people to read your blog in the first place. What were your goals for your blog? Does the post you're about to write have anything to do with those goals? If it doesn't and doesn't seem to fit with your chosen "voice", scrap it and move onto something else.

A "quality" blog post doesn't have to be hundreds of words long and incredibly deep. It can be a simple post of inspiration, or things that interest you. Just make sure that whatever you are posting reflects what YOU like, and contains content that you are actually interested in.

If you are out of ideas for blog topics, the best thing you can do is take a **break away** and clear your mind. Keep a pen handy and jot down little ideas and thoughts as they come to you. I do this a lot, and usually from one little word or jotted down note comes a full out blog post once I get down to it. A notebook is key if you are a blogger! I'm looking at one right now as I write this! Of course, you can always pick up a copy of my book, **365 Blog Topic Ideas** to keep on your desk!

All Set, Now What?: Attracting Visitors

So now that you've got your blog off to a rolling start, how do you attract more visitors? We've all been here before and sometimes it can feel like you're just not being heard out there in blog land.

Feature Other People

One way you can attract visitors is to feature other bloggers, businesses, or brands. Generally when you do this, the blogger or brand being featured will check out your post and hopefully send some people your way.

Etsy is a great place to find cool things that other people might not have seen before. Maybe you could feature some of your favourite creations and send a link to your blog post to the shop owner. They will appreciate the time you took to include their item in your post and will get acquainted with your blog at the same time. Businesses love free promotion and will usually be happy to share your post with their own followers!

Ask some of your favourite bloggers or business owners to do a little interview with you. I cannot guarantee that they will all say yes, but it's still worth a shot and you might be surprised at who would be willing to participate! Remember to relate the questions to your overall blog theme so it fits in!

Finally, an important thing to remember when trying to attract visitors is to make sure you don't come across as vain or self-concerned. **Always** genuinely support other bloggers and business owners and be friendly with everybody you come across. Always make sure you link back to the people you feature and give your own readers the opportunity to check them out as well. It's a two way street here, friends!

Giveaways

I'm a little bit on the fence about this one, because I have mixed opinions about giveaways. Yes, they are great for gaining some new "Likes" or followers, but do the new fans you gain actually stick around? Everybody loves free stuff and lots of people are quick to simply follow a blog for the sake of a giveaway and then unfollow them after it's over. I do a giveaway for my site sponsors once a month on my blog. Those giveaways are entirely for them... to get a little extra exposure and for their products to be seen.

If you want to jump on the giveaway bandwagon, you'll need some prizes. Generally business owners aren't going to want to donate anything if you don't have a following to back you up. **There has to be something in it for them too**. Start asking people you know if they'd like to participate in a small giveaway, for example, if you have a friend who makes hair accessories. Another thing you can do is offer your own prize. If you have your own shop, perfect! Some bloggers give away gift cards they've purchased for the sole purpose of giving away on their blogs. This might attract a wider range of visitors depending on where the gift card is from.

Whatever way you choose to go about it, make sure you set some ground rules for entries. Have the entrants follow you to enter, leave a comment, share your giveaway on Twitter... the list goes on. This is how building that following begins. Keep in mind though, that a percentage of those people who do enter will not always stick around afterwards. That's life, I suppose!

Social Media

We covered Social Networking already, but how can you use this to your advantage and attract visitors?

Once again, it's all about getting involved in the community. Visit other Facebook, Twitter, and social pages. See what other people are up to and get involved in their conversations. Blogging is very much like making new friends. How would you approach someone new in public? You wouldn't start your conversation off like "Oh hi, check out my blog I have a giveaway going on!"... Can you imagine?! That person would probably roll their eyes and walk away. Something to keep in mind here is to think about social media as though it is real life. Strange thought, isn't it!? We are so consumed by computers that we sometimes forget that there are real people behind the screens. Spark up real conversations with others as you would in real life and you'll find that things just flow better.

Another thing to remember to do is to **stay active** on social networks. This doesn't mean checking your Facebook Page once every two weeks to see if you have any new "Likes". Use it to your advantage and get out there! If someone visits your page and notices you haven't updated it in a month, why would they want to stick around? Keep it fresh with content and always current.

Follow Other Blogs

Like I said above, this is a two way street. If you want people to follow you, you've got to get out there and follow them, too. If you come across a blog you like, click that little Follow button to show your support. Comment on their articles and leave a link back to your site. I feel that it's ok to let a blogger know that you just stumbled upon their site and you really like their blog. There's nothing wrong with telling them that they've done a good job and have gained a new follower (you) because of it. Most of the time, that blogger will return the favour and check out your blog too. Without directly asking them to visit your blog, comment is more genuine and your link is there just in case they decide to click it.

Set a Goal

Goals are always great for pushing yourself forward. When I started out and my followers started growing, I made a secret goal with myself that I would attract **five** new followers a day. I started visiting hundreds of blogs, and reading probably more than I have ever read in my lifetime. Doing that allowed me to follow others and do just as I had suggested in the above paragraph. My five follower a day goal was working and I was excited!!

Pinterest

I have found Pinterest_to be an amazing source for attracting new visitors. In fact, traffic I get from Pinterest makes up about 50% of my sites stats. If you have an interesting blog post, tutorial, or pretty photos you want to share, pin your posts to Pinterest. When you post to Pinterest, your link is included on the image so when people click on it, they will go to your site. It always helps to add a little watermark to your images if you are worried about the credit being lost. Most of my tutorial images have "thewonderforest.com" written on them just in case.

Pinning other people's finds will also help gain your Pinterest followers. Just remember to always give credit to the original source when you are pinning something from somebody's website. Pin the **actual blog post** and not the main blog URL so others can find it easily if they need to.

Spend about an hour a day networking, Pinning, and making yourself seen. After trying your hand at these tasks, you should see a positive outcome. Just stick with it, I know that it can be frustrating sometimes if you don't see any growth happening right away, but just try harder! Visitors will come, but they won't magically find you.

Chapter Three
Engaging Readers
Show That You Care.

Now that you've got some followers, you've got to think about why they should stick around. When you're writing your blog posts, think about the fact that you are writing **to them**. Post topics that ask for opinions... Get your readers involved in some way. Show that you care that they are taking the time to read your blog.

I find that asking a question at the end of my post is always a conversation starter. Ask your readers what their take is on what you have just written about. Ask a specific question relating to your post. People are quicker to comment when there is an answer to be pondered, and honestly, the comments end up being more about quality than quantity as well. By that, I mean that there are less "Oh hi I love your blog!" type comments, and more thought-out, knowledgeable and interesting ones. Making people think about something is a great way for your blog to stick out in their minds as well.

Noticing your regular readers can benefit you as well. If you notice a "regular" on your blog, take the time to check out their site as well (if they have one) and reciprocate the love. Making them aware that you notice them and appreciate the time they take to visit your blog all the time can go a long way!

Visit other reader's blogs. If your readers or commenters have blogs, click on their link and check them out. Leave them comments back. They will appreciate it and know that you are a caring blogger who's not just in it to gain fame of some sort. If you happen to like one of their particular posts, share it with your own readers or followers!

Engaging Readers: Making Friends With Bloggers

I kind of don't really know where to start with this chapter because all of the blogger friendships I've made have just sort of happened. They weren't forced, and I didn't intentionally go out and try to make friends with them just to get in their "circle".

I think the most important thing to be aware of is that just like any real life friendship, it has to be sincere. You're not always going to get along with everybody in real life, just like you aren't going to get along with everybody on the internet. In real life, I am really choosy with my friendships. I think that I am the same way with blog relationships too.

I love the online friendships I've made and the behind-the-scenes emails I share with other fellow bloggers. It's nice to talk about blogging in general and have somebody understand what you mean! I have shared some deep secrets with some and have been overwhelmed with support. These relationships might even go deeper than some of my real life ones, odd as that sounds.

All of that said, you can't force a friendship. I truly believe that people just click, or they don't... and that's fine!

I "met" one of my online girlfriends after finding her blog for the first time. When I visited it, I just felt like this person was so real and already one of my friends. I decided to open up my email and shoot her a cute note. That email turned into many back and forth conversations and BAM an international friendship was born. That's really how it works, in a nut shell. You can't force these things, they will just happen... however, don't be afraid to let someone know that you think they are great if you really do feel that way! Whether they become your friend or not, you at least made someone happy for a while with some kind words.

Something I need to note here though: Don't be a kiss ass! Don't email somebody just because you want to get in their "circle" or to gain popularity for yourself. Bloggers who have been doing this a long time can see right through that and know that you're not being real. Also, it's not polite to ask for favours if you've never even spoken to the person before. That is pretty tasteless and will just get your email hit with the "delete" button. I even feel weird asking for anything from my blogger friends, even having known them quite some time.

Engaging Readers:
Negativity

As you travel down this road, you're more than likely going to run into a few "Negative Nancies". Fortunately, I haven't had to deal with many of them, but if you do, what should you do?

I think the best thing to do if someone leaves you a mean comment, is to ignore it and delete it. Negative commenters usually don't disclose their identities and like to post under "Anonymous" handles, so they don't give you a method of contact to hash it out with them. They say their piece, stir the pot, and leave.

One way you can stop the anonymity is to only allow registered users to comment on your blog. Your blog's settings have an option for who can comment, so be sure to check those out. If you continue to allow anonymous posters to comment, you're fueling their desire to leave you a negative comment.

Not everybody is going to agree with you, and that's ok. That's part of life. If someone feels the need to be negative in leaving their own opinion, don't feel badly. Everybody is entitled to their own opinion. If you feel the desire, let them know in a follow-up comment that you respect their opinion, or tell them "that's an interesting way of looking at it", for example. You acknowledge that they have a difference of opinion, but are not adding to their negativity and just accepting their comment for what it is.

I think it's necessary to kind of grow a thick skin if you're the sensitive type. The important thing to remember is to not get angry and loose it on somebody. You are a kind-hearted blogger, not a mean one. If you feel the need to retaliate and say your piece, you could just be adding fuel to the fire and encouraging a mean commenter to continue with their bashing. If you want to acknowledge it, acknowledge it in such a way that respects both opinions (even if you don't agree with theirs) and puts an end to it. Stop that Negative Nancy in their tracks and they won't be back.

Chapter Four
So, You're A Blogger...
Staying Current

Now that you've got a following and are taking this blogging thing seriously, you need to start thinking about staying current. By this, I mean that you need to keep your site fresh! Posting new content regularly is key, but how else can you make the most of your blog?

Don't Neglect Your About Page

Having an "About Me" page on your blog is a wonderful place to start. Visitors love finding out more about the person behind the blog, and this is the place to do it. An about page should include whatever information you want to share about yourself... things to help others get to know you better and learn a bit more about your blog in general.

My About page has everything from my job, to my relationship, pets, and more! I basically included everything on that page that I would want a new friend to know about me right off the bat.

Updating your About page every now and then is important. Why? Because we all change! Swap out some old photos with some new ones. Edit your content, or add some more! Linking to past posts in your About page is also a great way for visitors to find your past ramblings. For example, on my about page I talk about being engaged to my fiance who finally obtained his immigration status in Canada... The word "immigration" is linked to a past post where I talk all about our trials and frustrations with the immigration process. Doing this also helps with your search engine rankings. It helps search engines crawl through your site because they follow link after link.

Don't Forget About Quality

Now that you're blogging regularly, remember what you told yourself in the beginning about quality vs. quantity. Don't feel the pressure to post any old thing just to have a blog post for the day. Always make sure that your posts contribute something to your blog. If you've been keeping a notebook like we talked about earlier, you should have no problem staying current and having new things to talk about.

Start a Series

Starting a series on your blog is one way that you can stay current with your content. Creating a series will help readers stay interested in your content because they know that they can come back and hang out with you again on another given day. It's something to look forward to!

Tech Tuesday is a feature on my own blog that I started a while back. I feature digital content such as free downloads, product reviews for cool technologies, and other internet or tech based things. See if there is something that you can come up with that will encourage you to post on a certain day every week.

So, You're A Blogger...: Appreciate Your Readers

You didn't get where you are now by being self-concerned and vain, right? If you listened to anything I've said in this eBook, I sure hope not! Remember how you visited other blogs and commented? Well, other fellow bloggers are trying to do the same thing. Remember that you are all in the same boat!

Emailing or commenting an **old reader** is a great way to show that you appreciate them. I have personally emailed past commenters on my blog just to say hi. I don't forget about any of the people who have been so sweet to me along this journey, and it's important that you don't either. I can name dozens of my regular commenters off the top of my head... and whether they know that or not, it means the world to me that they find my life interesting enough to read about!

Those people take the time out of their day to catch up on what you're doing. The least you could do is send them a sweet note back, or comment on some of their own blog posts, just to let them know that "hey, I'm here and you're not just another faceless commenter".

Another thing that I always try to do is answer all of the emails I get. As you grow, this might become more of a daunting task, but even still I think it's important to not let them go ignored. Somebody spent their own time writing something to you, the least you could do is write back.

It's hard sometimes to sit down and reply all day long, but I do it for my readers. Sometimes it takes me a week or two (okay, sometimes a month if I'm honest) because my inbox is seriously nuts, but it will always get done.

So, You're A Blogger...:
Blog Advertising.

I know I know, some of you will jump right to this chapter because it's been on the top of your list for a while. Let me tell you something though, it's worth the wait. First of all, you cannot expect to have sponsors pay for advertising on your blog if you're new to this.

Like we talked about in the Blog Expectations chapter, you cannot expect to start making money right away. I've come to realize that in blog world, there is sort of an unspoken rule that if you have under 500 blog followers, you should not start advertising just yet. 500 seems to be a good rule of thumb, so you could continue working on building up that audience before you dive into the venture that is sponsorships., which we will cover later.

So, how do you start offering some kind of advertising on your blog? You swap! Yep, good old fashioned tradesies! When I first started looking for advertisers, I posted a blog about accepting button swaps. Here is what I posted:

Blog Banner Swap!

What is a banner swap? *It's when two blogs (mine, and yours!) swap sidebar banners with each other... Think of it as* **free advertising** *for a* **month!** *Right now, I am accepting "swapees" (new word) to be featured on my blog for a whole month! If you feel that your blog would be of interest to my readers, please email me dana@thewonderforest.com with subject line **"BLOG SWAP"** by July 25th and let me know:*

Your name
Your blog name
Your blog URL
and send a banner ad sized at 180px wide by 150px high.

If I feel that your blog is a good match for mine, I would love to feature your button on my site! I will only be selecting 10 or so banners... but **everyone** *is welcome to send me a submission! Once I choose them all they will go up! I will be placing this section closer to the top of my sidebar so you all get* maximum *exposure.*

What do you have to do? *All that is required is that you grab one of my buttons and put it in your blog sidebar too! This is a* swap *after all ;) I can create custom sized ones if you need.*

I also just created some brand new *banners that you can put on your blogs... just scroll down my right sidebar to check them out! They have transparent backgrounds so work well on any colour blog. Hope to hear from you soon!*

xo Dana

I got a great response and I had my first sidebar friends! I offered swapping for about 2-3 months before I branched out and actually started charging for my advertising services. That's all it takes, just a little time so that people can see you have people interested in having their banner on your site.

You can also email some of your fellow blogger friends and see if they would be interested in swapping banners with you for a month.

Something to keep in mind in regards to the swapping

though, is that you shouldn't ask a blog that has a significantly higher amount of followers than you. Remember, there has to be something in it for them too... and usually they will feel as though they're getting the short end of the stick, and you're getting free advertising on a bigger blog.

I've had to politely turn down some bloggers that have emailed me asking if I would like to swap and after checking out their site, I find that they have no audience, or 20-ish followers. I don't mean to sound rude here, but to me, that's just not fair for somebody who has worked their butt off building up their own audience. Bloggers that charge for their sponsorships should not be asked to swap unless you have an equal (or pretty even) amount of followers. That's just how it works, friends!

So, You're A Blogger...: Participation and Features

While traveling along this blogging road, you'll occasionally be stopped to ask to participate in giveaways, interviews, and features. So should you partake? I say, absolutely! Participating in any type of feature is going to help get your blog out there. Even if the blog you're featured on doesn't have a huge audience, it's still going to help you out. How you ask? Search engines, my friend!

In case you didn't know this, the more places your actual text link is shared on, the higher you will rank in search engines. Google sees your link at all of these different places and thinks to itself, "oh, this blog is being talked about! It must be important!" There is no downside to having your link posted in as many places as you can have it. So if you think that a blog is too "low-profile" for you to do an interview with, just remember that!

If you're a business, giveaways on other blogs or websites are a great way to drive traffic to your blog/facebook/shop, etc. It's always a good idea to ask the person hosting the giveaway if there will be certain requirements for the entrants, such as "liking" your Facebook page. Something to keep in mind is that you will be giving away actual product here. Don't let it blow your budget, nobody likes to give things away for free and not see any kind of return! While a giveaway is actually a type of free promotion for you, you're essentially paying for it with the cost of your giveaway prize. Which is fine in some cases, but be sure that the prize you're offering suits the blog that you're featured on.

By this, I mean that you shouldn't go giving away a $50 shop credit or something on a blog that only has a small amount of readers and traffic. There is not much return for you in doing that because the giveaway will not be shown to a very wide range of visitors. Choose your prizes wisely, and don't feel like you always need to participate in them either.

Features are more my cup of tea. Sometimes bloggers will ask to feature you, which is amazing because they will talk about you and share what you do with their own readers. It's free promotion, without having to give anything away or dip into your own pockets. Any opportunity you can get to be featured will help you out in the long run.

Guest posting is another option. Sometimes if you have some blog friends, they will ask to do guest posts, which essentially is you taking over their blog with your own post. Sometimes they will give you a topic to write about, other times they will leave it up to you. You can also offer guest posts to your own blog friends if you'd like to help them out as well and share them with your readers.

Any feature is a good feature. If you're trying to grow and expand your audience, being talked about is the utmost form of flattery!

So, You're A Blogger...: Advertising on Other Blogs

Something you'll need to consider during your blogging

ventures is whether or not you want to advertise your own site on other blogs. Many blogs offer sidebar advertising, or "sponsoring" opportunities and you should decide if you think your own blog could benefit from this.

Do some research.

Don't just randomly pick blogs to advertise on just because they offer blog advertising. You'll need to spend a little time and weed through dozens of potential blogs before settling on one, or a couple.

Is the blog targeting your same target audience?

If you buy an ad on a blog that is in a totally different category than your own, there won't be much benefit to advertising there. Try to keep your blog advertising within the same "niche".

How broad is the blogger's audience?

Check out their stats, followers, comments on posts, and overall reader participation. Do they have a Facebook page? A Twitter account? Do they share posts there? Additional social media accounts could mean more bang for your buck.

Does the blogger update their site often?

This is important because it relates to the amount of traffic the blogger is driving to their own website. If they aren't bringing in the traffic, they're not giving you the best possible exposure for your money.

Does the blogger interact with their readers?

I also find that this one is important. Some of the best traffic I've received from blogs are from those that interact daily with their visitors.

Does the blog offer any incentives for advertising?

Such as mentioning you in a featured sponsor post, or have giveaway opportunities? In other words, how will the blogger advertise YOU? (You are paying for advertising, after all!)

How much are you willing to spend?

Don't go nuts on buying up advertising spots without considering all of the above. Once you know which sites would be good matches for your own blog, think about how much you are willing to spend. Some bloggers offer discounts on advertising spots near the end of the month to fill up remaining space. Some others even offer discounts if you purchase multiple months of advertising. Take advantage of things like this if you can. Advertising cost will depend on each individual blog and the amount of traffic they get. If you think that a certain blog can help you gain traffic, how much is that traffic worth to you?

It's hard to say which blogs will generate the most traffic for your buck without diving in and testing some out yourself. You can always start with a small ad space and see how well that works for you before moving up to their larger spots with more features. Blog advertising seems to be hit or miss sometimes, but once you find those key sites that actually help generate new readers for you, hold onto them!

Chapter Five
Making Money With Your Blog Sponsorships.

Another thing many bloggers want to do is offer their own blog advertising. We talked a little bit about swapping with other blogs to get your sponsorships started, but now let's dive into the good stuff... how to make money from ads.

First of all, it's not always totally necessary, but you could always go by the 500 follower rule. Offering sponsorships really ultimately depends on whether you feel you have an established blog. This doesn't always depend on your follower count, so check your stats, the amount of comments you're receiving, how many new and returning commenters you're noticing, and whether or not you feel these things could help you launch a sponsorship program. If you did what I suggested and offered sponsorship swaps to start, you should have a pretty good idea of everything that's involved in hosting ads.

When you're ready to start accepting actual paying ads, where do you start?

Well, I started cheap. I offered ad spots from $5-$10 to start, and that really paid off. The price of your ads depends on how much traffic you receive, and how many followers from all of the different networking sites you have. As you grow, you can feel more comfortable raising your prices, but to start, the lower the better. You need to gain an interest before sticking a $100 price tag on an ad spot.

You'll also need to consider the fact that accepting sponsorships means more work on your plate. People are now essentially paying you to blog, so remember that and don't disappoint them! You will need to make time to set up the ads, email your sponsors for features, set up feature posts, giveaways, and get ready to promote them so they get what they're paying for. Remember what we talked about in the Advertising on Other Blogs chapter? Well, now you are that blog.

There are ad management sites like Passionfruit Ads that help with the scheduling and payment part. Definitely check it out if you're going to start accepting paid sponsorships. They are a paid service, but most bloggers don't mind paying it because it takes all of the headaches away from organizing your sidebar and managing payments. If you opt to handle this yourself, make sure you have an organizer handy and know your blog ad's stop and start times.

How Do You Get Sponsors?

How do you get people to sign up for sponsorships? Every month, many bloggers post a "sponsor call" which basically just states that they are accepting sponsorships for the following month, and lists all of the details. You will also want to set up a "sponsor" or "advertise" page that lists all of your site's information. I love it when blogs include their true stats so you can see exactly what you're getting when you sign up. Your sponsor page should include all of that information as well as what each ad size will include, and the price. Some bloggers do not disclose prices on their blogs which can be a bit of a turn off for some because it takes more effort to contact them and communicate back and forth. When I'm looking for places to advertise, I want to know right off the bat how much they charge and if they're worth my time. I don't want to have to email them, wait for a response, and save their email that includes pricing and info for a later date.

What You Should Not Do

Do not email other blogs asking them to sponsor yours. This is so unprofessional and looks like you're just in it for the money. It's like when people come knocking at your door asking for money. Any good sponsor will find you and decide for themselves if they'd like to advertise on your blog. If you are emailing them to suggest a potential swap or brand partnership, that's a different story.

Deciding What to Charge

This one is probably the toughest part of offering advertising. You can raise your prices as you grow, but to how much? I found it most helpful to just research a few other blogs that have the same amount of followers as you and check out their pricing structure. Generally, they all seem to be around the same ballpark.

Staying Organized

If you're not going to use Passionfruit Ads, you'll want to make sure you stay organized in other ways. Before Passionfruit, I kept everything in a notebook. I would write down the month and below that list all of the sponsors, their names, and what size ad they purchased. This was a really easy way of making sure I didn't forget anybody when the time came to put their ad up and email them about features and things.

Making Money With Your Blog: Adsense

Another way to accept advertising on your blog is to sign up for Google Adsense or other affiliate programs. Let's talk about Adsense first.

Now, being in the web design field, I have a lot of experience with Adsense. Adsense is an advertising network made by Google that hosts ads from people and companies that are signed up with their other advertising program, Adwords. The ads that display on your blog are usually completely keyword-driven, meaning that whatever keywords Google picks up on your blog, your Google ads will target.

Some companies customize their Adwords to only display on certain blogs or websites that they choose. Basically, they pay a fee for each ad that is clicked on. In turn, you make a small commission for hosting that ad and generating the click for them. This money is held in your Adsense account.

Blogger makes it easy for you to set up Adsense with your blog. Just click on the Monetize link in your dashboard and it will walk you through the steps.

Before you continue though, there are some things you need to know.

First of all, it can take a while to generate any revenue through Adsense. You might only receive 1 cent per click. Aside from that, Adsense only pays you once you reach $100 in your account. Making actual money with Adsense depends on a couple of factors: how much traffic your site gets, and the placement of your ads, which I will talk about later.

I do not recommend anyone who does not receive decent traffic to advertise with Adsense. It just doesn't make much sense. It would take FOREVER to reach the $100 threshold and your site would just look messy with Adsense ads all over the place. #1 pet peeve is when I go to other blogs and all you see is advertising everywhere. Ugly Google ads that stand out everywhere you look. How is this attracting new potential sponsors or readers?

If you ARE receiving decent traffic, you might want to consider setting up some small Adsense ads. Yes, I said **small**. You'd be surprised at how many people click on little text links as opposed to big "in your face" skyscraper sidebar ads.

Blogger lets you display Adsense ads easily with their little widgets. You can place them in your sidebar, in between posts, and in your site's RSS feeds. I recommend setting them up in your feeds because they don't interfere with the look of your blog, and can be viewed by many using feed readers. It's just a little extra money making spot.

Wherever you decide to put your ads, they should **blend in** with the rest of your blog. People are more likely to click an ad (remember: clicking = more money) if they think it's a part of your design. Sneaky? Maybe, but it's what's proven and I can vouch for the fact that it works. Place a strip of text link ads below your posts and make the link colours the same as your blog's link colours. If you make sure the styles match your blog, this always helps. Blogger makes it easy to do so. If you don't use Blogger, you can easily set the styles and format your ads in the

Adsense dashboard.

Once you have Adsense set up, don't think that you're automatically going to start making tons of money. Like I said, it takes a lot of clicks and pageviews to make money. And don't even think about clicking your own links or ads over and over again, because Google tracks this and will shut you right down... they will actually ban you from Adsense forever. (trust me, my friend tried this and can never use Adsense again!). You might only make 1 cent one day, or maybe nothing. However other days, you might make $2. As your blog grows and if your ads are placed properly, you may start seeing a good increase in the amount of clicks you get. So just remember what you learned here and don't hold high expectations for Adsense.

Making Money With Your Blog: Affiliate Programs

Affiliate programs are advertising programs that you sign up through a special network. There are many of them out there, Google Affiliate Network, RewardStyle, Commission Junction... Believe me I've tried them all. With an affiliate network, you sign up and then apply for accounts with each individual advertiser. In some cases they have to approve your site before you are allowed to place their banners on your site.

The largest affiliate networks have huge companies backing them, and each one sets a certain percentage they will pay you per sale. That means, if you generate a sale for them by someone clicking a link on your site and purchasing something, they pay you, but usually only after that sale has closed (7-30 days).

 The thing with Affiliate programs is, you aren't paid per **click** like you are with something like Adsense or other pay-per-click ad networks. You are only paid per **SALE**. Like I said above, that means that if someone clicks on your affiliate link and buys something, you will get a percentage of that sale. This could mean more money if you're good at pushing products to people or have a company that relates to your blog very well, but it could also mean a waste of time if not.

Affiliate networks put a threshold on how much you have to earn before you are paid. Some are $50, others are $100. Besides that, they also have wait times after you reach that threshold. Each program is different, but in some cases you have to wait an additional 60-90 days before you see that money in your bank account.

The trick is to not advertise things that you wouldn't personally buy. It's all about staying genuine with your blog, right? I will only display banners/links to shops that I actually do buy from, and products that I have talked about and/or use.

Is It Worth It? It really depends on how well you are able to promote a product or company. Sometimes you could spend all of your energy trying to advertise these sites and products and the reward is just not that great. Other times, however, you could make ten times as much as with pay-per-click ads. If you are able to easily promote products through your posts, I say go for it! You'll never know how much money you can make unless you try, right?

Making Money With Your Blog: Product Reviews

Another thing you might want to consider is whether or not you will accept product for review. Accepting product for a review means that a person or company can send you some of their own product and will expect you to post about it.

I suggest before doing this that you lay down some ground rules, because things can get a little out of hand otherwise. First, if you have an "advertise" or "sponsorship" page on your blog, you can add in a little something about product reviews in there. State whether or not you are willing to do product reviews. If you are, will your product reviews be reserved specifically for sponsors? Or can anybody and everybody send you product to check out?

I started with accepting anything, just to get some other businesses heard on my blog, but I quickly noticed that it was getting a little crazy. People emailing me asking to review their products regularly, and while that is nice and all, I didn't want my blog to turn into a huge advertising site. I soon changed my terms so that only sponsors of my site can submit product for review... however if I really like something, I'll post about it whether they're a sponsor or not.

If you are going to accept product from people, state that you only review products that suit the style of your site and that everything has to be approved by you before sending. In other words, you pick out what you want to review. I only review things that I love... and that's SO important. Things that I would personally purchase. Don't accept anything for review just to get free stuff and then post about it if you weren't totally in love with it. You're misleading your readers in to possibly purchasing something they **thought** was recommended by you. (Not cool.)

So if you've received a product for review, what do you do? You try it out! You see if you love it. If you do, follow through with your end of the bargain and post about it. Make sure you state in your post that an item was "courtesy of" that business. If you live in the US, by law you have to state on your blog that you received an item for free.

When you write your post, it's always important to link back to the business/person that sent you your freebies. The whole point of them sending you product to begin with is to drive traffic to their own shops! So be nice and link back to them :)

If you start taking multiple review items, make sure you keep track of them all. I use a notebook for all of my blog-related things. Jot down who sent it to you, when you received it, what it was, and give yourself a deadline for posting about it. As a business having sent products to other blogs for review, I can tell you that it's torture waiting for a review to be posted! Stay on top of everything and you'll be just fine!

Making Money With Your Blog
Sell Your Services

Your blog is a money-making tool just waiting to be used. Once you have the traffic, you can use it to your benefit. If you have a service or product to sell, highlight it on your blog!

Blogs have come a long way. They are no longer just these personal havens full of nothing but journal entries. They are online venues for making sales and the potential for selling your services or products is huge. My sales for my own shop have increased ten-fold just by simply having a blog with a link to my store on it.

I've had such a great response selling my services on my blog too. Sure I have the web design background, but I never would have thought I would be selling custom blog designs, or even this eBook on my site... but you know what? I never would have if I didn't put myself out there and at least give it a shot!

If there's one thing my family and friends know about me, it's that I know how to make money. I have no idea where this skill comes from, but I can see a money making opportunity in everything. The key is to come up with a good idea if you don't already have a service to offer.

I've seen bloggers selling everything from consulting services to courses to clothing items from their own closets. Why not, right?!

Once you have a service or product to "pitch" to your readers, it helps to share your knowledge of the service or product in your blog posts. I don't mean that every blog post has to contain something about your service, I just mean that it helps if readers can actually see that you know what you're talking about every so often, and in turn that generates more sales for you. Demonstrate your knowledge about the service or show that product off in your own unique and stylish way!

As always, once you start selling things on your blog, don't be pushy about it. If every post you have says something about what you're selling, your readers will get bored and think you're only in this game to make money. Hopefully by now that's not the case and you actually love blogging! Place a graphic link to your product/service in your sidebar somewhere highly visible. Do one post each month about new products you have to offer or your latest clients.

It's time to get crafty and see what you can come up with. Put that beautiful brain to good use!

Closing

Now that your head is full of information and what has worked for me, I hope that you can continue along this blogging path and become happy and successful at what you do. I truly hope that what you've read here can be applied to your blog to help make it the best it can be!

The purpose of this eBook was to encourage you to improve and grow. One thing you must never forget, however, is to always enjoy what you do. If your heart is "all-in" this blogging game, then give it your best shot and work towards your goals. Only you are responsible for your successes!

So where do you go from here? Try putting some of these tips into action and track your progress. By now, you should have a little notebook handy and it should start filling up with ideas and blog-related writings.

Blogging is not for everyone, which is also important to remember. It's not a get-rich-quick solution or anything of the like. It is a way for you to share your thoughts and findings with the world, and hopefully by now you've come to realize your love for it.

I wanted to thank you for taking the time to read this eBook and supporting my own little dream. Because of you, I have been able to reach another of my own goals!

Have fun, and be yourself.

Dana Fox

ABOUT THE AUTHOR

Dana Fox is a Canadian blogger, entrepreneur, and artist with a passion for creativity. She launched her blog, Wonder Forest, in early 2011 and quickly gained a following. With the simple goal of taking her blog to new heights, Dana documented what worked for her, and what didn't. That documentation is this very book, Blog Wonderful.

You can find out more about Dana, Wonder Forest, and her many other projects over on her official blog: http://www.thewonderforest.com.

Need blog topic ideas? Check out her other book, **365 Blog Topic Ideas on Amazon!**

Printed in Poland
by Amazon Fulfillment
Poland Sp. z o.o., Wrocław